Enough is Enough

What is in "Your" S.H.O.E.?

To the Barcs Family

Dr. Ray Charles

Table of Contents

Foreword

By Lisa Nichols

Dr. Ray and I have a friendship that stems back seven years. We not only have a friendship but a relationship that is by divine design. We were introduced to each other by a mutual friend, and from that, trust became the foundation of our friendship. I affectionately call him "my brother from another mother." Not as a cliché or a phrase that was coined, but as truth. Dr. Ray is my brother, my friend, and one whom I can fully trust. I can count on him to be whatever I need at the moment. A shoulder to cry on, an ear to lend, a voice of reason, a heart of understanding. He selflessly offers the guidance of wisdom, the strength of a supporter, and a place of safety.

Dr. Ray, author, entrepreneur, and business coach, left a six-figure income to reset from ground zero. His mantra is "keep investing in people." In his book, *Enough is Enough: What's in Your S.H.O.E.?,* he pulls back the curtain on his life and exposes his own stumbling blocks, those things in his S.H.O.E. that hindered his progress in both his business and personal life.

This book embodies the core values and character of Dr. Ray. It speaks to our Spirit and shows us to listen to that voice, the inner voice that guides us on the right path. What path? It is 7:55am. Your meeting starts at 8:00am, and your reserved conference room is not available. What kind of Spirit do YOU show up with? In each chapter, Dr. Ray shows us to be accountable to the man/woman in the mirror. He challenges us to come face-to-face with habits that are actually holding us back from our full potential. The spirit of confidence. Or arrogance? Is there a thin line between the two? Or a bold one? Dr. Ray shows us how he separated the two. Through anecdotal illustrations, he proclaims: if the S.H.O.E. fits, then wear it! If not, find out what hinders your walk.

What *is* your S.H.O.E.? There is only ONE way to find out. Turn the page.... I

present to you Dr. Ray Charles' Enough
is Enough: What's in Your S.H.O.E?

~Lisa Nichols

Introduction

Why Now?

I decided to write this book because of
the agony and triumph that I and many of
my colleagues have experienced in
building our respective businesses and
careers. The pain stemmed from the fact
that we were all skilled in our craft, we
had years of experience under our belt,
we were confident in our ability because
of the intelligence we had amassed, yet
we were not gaining the traction for
acceleration and growth in our respective
fields. Sound familiar?

Success is the point at which skills, experience, and intelligence intersect. At least, that is what we were told. Yet no one told us that there are different dimensions of skills (e.g. social skills and technical skills), different dimensions of intelligence (e.g. general intelligence and emotional intelligence, aka "EQ"), and different dimensions of experience (e.g. natural experience and spiritual experience).

Oh, did I mention that we were also confident in our professional development journey, but no one forewarned us that to make this transition from intrapreneur (an employee who operates with the mindset of an entrepreneur) to a full-fledged entrepreneur required an investment in one's personal development and authenticity?

So, let my long road lead to your shortcut. What took me years to discover can take you an hour or less; simply from reading this book. I am going to share with you practical knowledge, lessons from my life experience (the good, the bad, and yes, the ugly).

There's no need for the both of us to go through the pain and suffering. My goal is to uncover many of the gremlins (whose sole purpose is to hold our feet from stepping into our predestined path to victory), as well as to share some of the breakthrough strategies.

So, Why Now?

We are living in a time where people are drowning in information yet starving for wisdom and knowledge. Accessibility to information is at an all-time high. I was one of those drowning; always feeling as though I did not have enough information to take the leap, always feeling as though I was not good enough, not qualified enough, not certified enough....until the day came when I finally said, "Enough is Enough."

12

You know, sometimes you will say something, and the moment you say it you realize, "Wow, this is more profound than I thought." Well, this was one of those moments. I thought I was saying, "Enough is Enough," from a place of frustration, but when the words came out of my mouth they had a totally new meaning and perspective. Instead of "ENOUGH is enough," I heard, for the first time, "Enough IS Enough." No matter where I was in my journey, I was enough. As I embraced that thought and mindset, the stars started to line up. Doors suddenly started to open. I started showing up not just as enough, but as more than enough.

From that day to the present, I have committed myself to take the information in my head, channel it into my heart, and walk it out in my feet. I was translated from the zip code of next to the zip code of now.

When I made that shift from next, from someday, to now (not just once, but on a daily basis), my entire life changed. I was transformed from a state of need to a state of choice and abundance. I no longer had to wait until I got to a certain place to share my story. I recognized that my story was history in the making. I was no longer living a life to leave a legacy— I was living my legacy, NOW.

14

What do you want to be known for?

The answer to that question was deposited in our DNA at birth, and some would say even before birth.

Like a player on the bench hollering, "Put me in coach!" our DNA cries out to our consciousness, "Put me in! Take me off the bench of your Spirit, and put me in your SHOE so that I can walk out this divine assignment."

So, before you read any further, write down on a blank sheet of paper the answer to this question: "What do you want to be known for?"

In the following pages, I will share with you four characteristics that I've discovered about our DNA (Distinct Natural Ability). Each of these characteristics, once actualized, makes its way into our shoe and propels us into a dimension far above hindrance and saboteurs.

Chapter One:
What's in "Your" S.H.O.E.—
Spirit

In this chapter, we examine the first element of your DNA in YOUR S.H.O.E. — Spirit.

What's amazing about the word "Spirit" is it is often framed in the context of religion when in fact, it has NOTHING to do with religion. I was blown away when I first came into the understanding of the true meaning of the word "spirit." It actually means life (as in breath of life.) It means position (as in mental disposition). The word spirit also means identity.

Let's examine the latter meaning - Identity

How many people do you know that are pursuing careers, imitating others, walking out other people's paths, placing their role model's feet in their shoes, while the spirit of the man/woman that is showing up each and every day is a false identity?

So, when the question is asked, "What spirit is in YOUR shoe?" it's really a check-in call. It's a check-in call to self, saying not only to wake up, but wake up and live.

It's a reality check, a beckoning call to self, saying, "Self, how are you showing up?"

I remember facilitating a leadership workshop where I posed a question to the audience: "So, tell me, what do you do?"

One of the attendees who happened to have a medical response dog with her in the class, shot up her hand, beaming forth with excitement. "I am the director of the local branch of the Humane Society."

I looked to her with a smile of acknowledgement, smiling at her service dog. "That's your role, your title if you will, but what do you really do?" I asked.

There was a deafening silence in the room, then she said, with far greater volume in her voice, "I give voice to those who cannot speak for themselves."

I responded, "Ahh, that's what you really do; that's what you are known for."

When was the last time you asked yourself that simple question? What do I really do?

Oh, by the way, if you have not already realized, this book is filled with simple truths. This is the type of question where we should have a few names on speed dial. Why? Because we may not like the answer to these self-reflective questions, and we just might need some words of wisdom and counsel.

But here is the good news, whether we realize it or not. Victory stems from the cellular forces in our DNA. If you're breathing in oxygen and breathing out carbon dioxide, if you are reading this book, then I have a very simple message for you. As admirable as it is to pursue victory, you and I were not designed to pursue victory. No. We were designed to operate from a place of victory. From a place where enough IS enough.

Victory is our Divine Footprint.

"Easy for you to say, Dr. Ray. You don't know my situation!" Well, the only part of that statement that is true is, I do not know your situation. But what I do know is that:

Every situation produces words

Every word produces thoughts

Every thought produces ideas

Every idea produces opinions

Every opinion produces feelings

Every feeling produces decisions

Every decision produces actions

Every action produces habits

Every habit produces convictions

Every conviction produces character
(identity, spirit)

Every character produces spiritual
influence

Every level of Spiritual influence
determines our destiny

24

So, at the end of the day, is it about the situation, or is it about the character and spiritual influence that is in your S.H.O.E.?

I remember six months after answering the call to be a Spiritual coach to leaders, I came across an ad in a business journal that read, "How to grow Spiritually while growing a multi-million-dollar business." Boy, was I super excited. When I read the ad, I said, "Yes! This is just for me!"

The ad was highlighting the final workshop of a five-day venture capital convention in Dallas, Texas. I thought it would be great to attend this convention, just to hear the speaker at this final workshop. But I immediately discarded the idea because of the price tag of the event. I heeded the Spiritual influence of doubt and unbelief that said, "You cannot afford it."

However, in the ensuing days, another message kept coming back to me. "What if you call and ask if you could get a discount for attending the final workshop, not the entire convention?"

Several days later, I acquired the courage (with knees knocking and teeth chattering) to place the call. Once connected, I announced my name and my interest in attending the final workshop. The person on the line kept

26

saying, "Wait a minute, THE Dr. Ray Charles? The Spiritual Coach?"

I responded, "Yes, I am Dr. Ray Charles, and yes, I am a spiritual coach." The gentleman then said, "Sir, we have been wanting to get in contact with you for months. You were referred to us, but we misplaced your contact information. If you look at the ad, you will notice it says, 'mystery speaker'."

With one hand on the phone and the other hand on the newspaper ad, I looked, and sure enough, it said "mystery speaker." The gentleman then said, "Sir, the mystery speaker at this conference is you." My jaw dropped! He continued,

"We were running out of time in going to print so on the integrity of the person who referred us, we decided to post the ad, believing and trusting that someway, somehow, we would get in contact with you!"

In that very moment, every influence of doubt, disbelief, low self-esteem, which almost talked me out of making the call, evaporated.

This was a watershed moment. It taught me that though we are surrounded by competing sounds, (sounds that rival against our true identity), as long as we are alive, the sound of our authentic spirit will not rest and will continue to nudge at us until our true identity emerges.

So, what's your sound? Is it a sound of "Winners never quit, and quitters never win"? Is it a sound of "I can, no matter what it looks like"? If it is, it will reveal itself in your spiritual influence. You'll start showing up differently. As long as you are following that authentic sound deep within, you will witness your Spiritual Influence growing from one dimension to the other (see below).

sions of Influence

1: Model

Level 2: Motivate

Level 3: Mentor

Level 4: Multiply

Regardless of your current age, I want you to do this quick exercise. Divide your age by 10. So, if you are 30, your answer is 3. Now answer this simple question. What sounds of influence have been resonating within you for each of the past decades you have been on the earth? Each of those sounds represents different stages of influence (Level 1-4 above) that you have walked.

Our Spiritual influence grows in spite of our imperfection.

It was fall 2001, approximately 5:30 AM on a foggy and dark Chicago morning. I was getting my final round of sleep when I heard my inner voice say to me, "Get up, I have something to say to you on the bike/jogging trail."

I said to myself, "This cannot be real. I must be dreaming."

Moments later, I heard it again, only this time louder, "Get up!"

With that I found myself negotiating with my inner voice. "Can you just say it to me in my bed?" That question generated no response. And so, with that silent treatment, I knew it was real.

I dragged myself out of bed, suited up with my jogging apparel, and made my way to the bike trail. An hour went by, heavy fog, no one in sight, and no conversation from within. Moments later I saw someone at a distance walking towards me. We greeted each other with a "Good morning," and kept going our separate ways.

Several footsteps later the young lady turned around and said to me, "Are you Dr. Ray Charles?"

Before I could say a word, I said in a whisper, "God is this it ….. Is this the conversation you wanted to speak to me?"

After acknowledging that I was Dr. Ray, she blurted out (and I mean loudly), "I knew it was you! I saw you on the ABC television special on coaching. Do you have a business card?"

Now, I'm saying to myself, "Lady, it's 6:00 AM. Who walks the trail at 6:00 AM in the morning with business cards?" Before I could answer her, I instinctively placed my hands in the pockets of my sweatpants and there was one, not so crisp, business card.

That was the extent of any conversation I had that morning on the bike trail. On my way back home I continued the inner dialogue, "Are you kidding me? Was that it? That's why you woke me up at 5:30 in the morning, to greet a stranger so she could let me know she saw me on ABC television?"

Three months later my cell phone rang. The voice on the other line said, "Dr. Ray, you may not remember me but we met several months ago, very early in the morning, on a bike trail."

At that point, I had totally forgotten about the "GET UP AND GET DRESSED, I have something to say to you on the bike trail," conversation I had in bed with God.

The young lady went on to say, "I'm not sure if you are an author, but I happen to know a publisher who is looking for someone who is bilingual in both faith and business, and I thought of recommending you, if you're interested. It's an Anthology featuring Dr. Robert Schuller, Dr. Tony Campolo, and Jennifer O'Neill. The publisher is looking for someone who can fill the last chapter of the book, 'Conversations on Faith.'"

My jaw dropped. I felt both excitement and remorse all at the same time. I was excited for the new opportunity, but remorseful for heeding the spiritual influence of doubt yet again, and being downright disrespectful to the voice of God. It was the voice of God within, beckoning me to get up from my sleep on that dark, foggy, fall morning and to make my way to the trail. In spite of my insolence, in spite of my imperfection of reluctance, my spiritual influence began to expand.

Since that encounter, I have come to realize that the only spiritual influence that belongs in my shoe, the only one that can transport me to my destiny is the Spirit of faith.

It was the Spirit (sound) of faith that broke through the chatter, transporting me from an idea to an action. I called the conference organizer to attend as a fan, only to be promoted from a fan to a player (the closing conference speaker.)

It was the Spirit of faith that brought me to my first Best Seller. And as I look through the rear-view mirror of life, it was the Spirit of faith that brought me from a career in chemical engineering to now, a calling in mindset engineering.

This Spirit of faith is standing eagerly ready in our shoes, awaiting its command to walk out (execute) our divine playbook. But here is the thing: in order to have this spirit of faith in our shoes, we must make the mental shift from being a FAN to being a PLAYER. You see, a fan is:

F - Full of knowledge

A - Always Analyzing

N - In neutral

No FAN has ever scored a touchdown. Because the fan is in the stands, and the goal is in the field.

But a player is one who:

P - Pursues

L - Leads

A - Acts

Y - Yields to what's best for the team

E - Empowers, Enrolls, Enchants, Endows

R - Receives the play calling from his/her coach (who in our case, is the voice of our conscience).

What if I had not heeded the inner voice (the play calling from my inner coach) and opted for the more favorable path (an additional hour of sleep)? Chances are I would not have discovered my passion for writing.

So today, you may not be writing a chapter on 'Conversations on Faith,' but every step you take is an opportunity for your life to be walked out and modeled (patterned after) by someone else, so that they can in turn build their spirit of faith.

Every spiritual influence portrays a unique story.

We each live our unique story. As we play our role by walking out our predestined purpose in the spirit of faith, there are a few questions you should consider as the actor/director of your film.

What is it you want your viewers to consider and internalize after they have seen your story?

If you were to critique your character in your story, would you like what you see?

If you were to name the top three characters in your film (other than you) who would they be?

What is the major plot (conflict) in your film?

How has your character's way of being transformed as you compare the present scene to the opening scene?

People are watching your story, whether you realize it or not.

The impact of your story grows with each level of your spiritual influence, in spite of the pebbles that are in your shoes.

Chapter Two:
What's in "Your" S.H.O.E. - Habits

Today my wife and I live a life of abundance. We choose when to work. We take several months off every year to focus on ministry and mission. We invest in our relationships and the relationship of our loved ones, without a care for physiological needs. We do this because we have changed some of the habits that are in our shoe. But it was not always that way.

I vividly remember times where I dreaded the thought of going home. As a former risk management consultant, I would apply the first principle of risk management: avoidance (avoid arguing, bickering, name calling, finger pointing, etc.) at all costs.

44

It was only when I realized that I was avoiding internal conflict with myself and my God that true change began to occur. I awoke to the dysfunctional habits (e.g. saying, "I'm ok, it's just who I am," etc.) that I was walking out on a daily basis.

In September 2017, my wife and I will be celebrating our 30-year wedding anniversary. However, I remember in year two she said something to me that was another watershed moment, a turning point if you will, that set me on the course to change my communication habits.

You probably want to know what she said, correct?

In the second year of our marriage, my wife looked at me and said, "You know, wives leave their husbands for a lot of reasons. They leave their husbands for domestic violence, for infidelity, drug addiction, etc., but do you know what I will leave you for if you do not change?"

Before I could answer, I said to myself, "No she did not say, what I will leave you for. This isn't just a complaint, this is a train that has already left the station, and the only person that can seemingly stop this train is me."

I started going through my mental checklist (domestic violence, infidelity, drugs) and nothing was checked, so what could she possibly be talking about? I finally and confidently asked, "So, what would you leave me for?"

Her next two words shook me to the core. She said, "Your arrogance!"

Yikes, arrogance! In an instant I had a man in the mirror moment:

"I'm starting with the man in the mirror
I'm asking him to change his ways
And no message could have been any clearer
If you want to make the world a better place
Take a look at yourself, and then make a change."

No message could have been any clearer than those two words my wife spoke to me.

As if I needed a confirmation of that message, a few weeks later, I began the journey of pledging for my fraternity. The very first day I overheard some of the brothers saying, "We're going to break him down, he is an arrogant son of a gun."

Without breaking any fraternal confidentiality, let me just say that the next six weeks of pledging contributed greatly to the distillation of my arrogant habits and ways that were in my shoes (ways that I was walking out on a daily basis).

I became another man. I entered the fraternity for social gain, but ended up gaining the treasure of humility, servanthood, and compassion. I did not know the dysfunctional habits of arrogance and cockiness that dwelt in my shoes. Instead of trying to throw it out the window, I walked it slowly down the steps, chipping away bad habits, each day, by submitting to godly counsel.

What habits are in YOUR shoe?

Mark Twain once said:

You can't break a bad habit by throwing it out the window. You've got to walk it slowly down the stairs.

In the first few years of my marriage, I tried to break the bad (dysfunctional) habits I adopted from my dad. As a matter of fact, I entered the marriage with one goal, and one goal only: to be the complete opposite of what I saw in, and even more importantly, what I heard about my dad since infancy.

As a child, I was my mom's "shadow." I witnessed her tears, torrential complaints towards and about my dad, heard her regrets, etc. What I did not know was, the more I tried to break those habits by throwing them out the window, the more my father's feet were placed in my shoe. I was walking out his reality, playing a role from one of the early scenes of his life's movie.

The more I tried to be a good husband, the closer I got to divorce court! In the midst of one of my heated arguments with my spouse, I literally saw myself going down a downward spiral.

The habits that you avoid are the things that linger.

It was as if I were translated into a trance. In the midst of the argument, I could see my wife's mouth moving, but I could not hear a word. Then the next thing I heard shook me to the core. I heard, the voice within, saying to me: "This issue is not between you and your spouse. This issue is between you and Me. You're living a lie. You're trying to be someone who you're not. You are not your anti-father. If only you would receive the call I have placed on your life (and walk it out), you will see that most of your relational conflicts would begin to disappear."

And so, in that very moment, I made the decision to become another man. Notice I did not say, I became another man, I made the decision to become another man.

I laid down my black robe of a judge (judging my spouse without having the full context,) I laid down the eraser (the futile attempts of avoiding my wife from experiencing what my mother went through.) Instead, I became a ready pen, ready to write my true story on the heart of my loved ones.   But the full manifestation of that would take years of refinement.

Some people call these turning points. Tipping points. Transitional moments. Whatever point they are, what I want you to know is that each one of us, at some point or another, will be faced with these watershed moments whose sole purpose (like a bowling lane bumper) is to get us back on our intended and predestined course. The more we are bumped back on course, the more we will be committed to develop new and improved habits to stay the course.

So...

What habits are in YOUR shoe?

Are they serving you?

Are they drawing you closer to your life's mission?

Changing your habits will not come with an operating manual.

After I left my job, in pursuit of my calling, I found myself walking in no-man's land, (a place of the unknown) without a step-by-step plan. Although I won the personal battle, I was now dealing with the professional battle. I went from overcoming arrogance and the avoidance of a false identity to the battle of regret and anguish because of deception (I kept focusing on what I had lost, as opposed to what I had gained—I had not fully embraced my calling).

I would often say to myself, "Have you lost your mind, sacrificing your dream home, your family stability, your financial security, everything you built?" What I did not know during the early days of asking these probing, condemning, judgmental, questions was that the habits that got me here, won't get me there.

You see, the habits that got me to the pinnacle of my career, (prior to answering the call) were based on information (knowledge, science, etc.). But the habits that would take me on my new "INVENTURE" were based on revelation.

The more I compared my "now" self with my "then" self, the more I opened my heart and mind to anguish, regret and heaviness.

A week after I left my profession to pursue my calling, my wife hosted a huge "Exodus" party at our home. It was fully catered and we had over one hundred of our close friends there. It was as though she had already had it all lined up and was simply waiting for me to follow through on answering my call. Still, the habit of guilt and shame in my shoe lingered, prompting me to ask myself, "What makes you think you are qualified for this call? You have no experience in coaching, you have no one to model after. And why now? Why not after you've established a sizable nest egg and your family is well provided for?"

The months that followed were dark seasons. I appreciated the love and support I received from my spouse and Spiritual coaching clients, but the thought of being a failure was such a regular visitor, it assumed its own real estate in my mind, reminding me continually of the saying, "If any Man provide not for his own, and especially for those of his own house, he has denied the faith, and is worse than an infidel."

What was it that caused me to break through this debilitating cycle? What was it that caused me to rise from the "shame and guilt?"

Changing the habits that were in my shoe!

Some of the changed habits included:

Speaking | Setting | Settling | Sowing

Speaking what I believe, versus speaking what I knew.

Setting process goals, versus production goals.

Settling once and for all, that what was before me was far greater than what was behind me.

Sowing in tears and reaping in joy— supporting others from a pure heart, without a care or thought of reciprocity.

Speaking

Leaving behind nights of terror and fear

I rise

Into a daybreak that's wondrously clear

I rise ... Maya Angelou

I started to live from the inside out as opposed to the outside in. The more I practiced this new habit, the more my self-actualization muscles were built. Once my mind aligned with what I believed in my heart and I practiced speaking from that place, my action automatically followed. I started showing up with a greater degree of confidence.

Setting

Unlike my corporate experience, where annual goals were set based on historical trends and analysis of known numbers, I started setting process goals, intrinsic and chunk sized, based on value and character. My goals began focusing on leadership character (below the iceberg) versus skills (above the iceberg).

The late Stephen Covey speaks of this as the difference between production (above the iceberg) and production capability.

Settling

I remembered it like it was yesterday. I was celebrating my 50th birthday in my favorite vacation spot, St. Maarten. While having some delicious French crepes on the beach, and feeling the sand and water from the shores slowly retreating from my feet, I heard a still voice saying, "You are now on the 50-yard line. What you have left behind is pale in comparison to what you have and will continue to gain. Just as the waters retreated from Noah's Ark, causing everyone in the ark to be saved, so is the water and sand retreating from your feet this very moment."

From that day to today, I settled once and for all, Enough IS Enough.

"Leaving behind nights of terror and fear I rise."

Sowing

Finally, the fourth, and possibly the most pivotal habit to be transformed from my shoe was my economy. Prior to accepting my calling, in my corporate life, I lived out of my earnings. Today, I live out of my assets, and my greatest asset is the Voice of God.

That one shift in habits has totally transformed my:

Words

Thoughts

Ideas

Feelings

Decisions

Actions

Habits

Conviction

Character

Destiny

So, as we bring this chapter to a close, ask yourself, once again, what habit in YOUR shoe is keeping you in the realm of the ordinary, holding you back from the elevated state of your destiny?

Chapter Three:
What's in "Your" S.H.O.E. - Observant

Muhammad Ali once said, "It isn't the mountains ahead to climb that wears you out, it's the pebble in your shoe."

Discerning (observing) the difference between the mountain and the pebble is significant to our forward motion.

Notice the champ never said the "pebbles." So, this pebble is singular, though its purpose is varied. Its purpose includes:

Causing you to limp

Be an irritant in your walk

Preventing you from putting your own weight in your shoe

So, what is it that has caused you to limp? What is it that has been the irritant in your walk? And, most importantly, knowing that the words weight and glory have the same root meaning, what is it that has prevented your true light, your full weight in your shoe (your glory) from being ushered into the world?

Let's contrast the pebble with the mountains.

Unlike the pebble, the mountains are not intended to harm or impede us. Like a military obstacle course (and we each have an obstacle course, whether we realize it or not), the mountains we climb in our life's journey are there:

To simulate the real battle when we enter our promised land.

So that we may overcome what will be our natural reaction when we are in danger.

To give us mental toughness (to cause us to fight, not flight, when danger is all around us).

Observing and distinguishing the difference between the pebble and the mountains is crucial to the fulfilment of our divine purpose. Now here is the thing. The pebble does not have the power to deny us, but can derail us by providing enough enticement. So, if we aren't aware (once again showing the significance of observing) we will surrender our power and voluntarily take ourselves out of the game.

Never in a million years would I have predicted in 1982, when I enrolled as a freshman in college, that my journey (walk) would take me from chemical engineering to "mindset" engineering. Today, if someone were to introduce me they will say something like:

"Dr. Ray is a mindset engineer. He has learned how to use his knowledge in engineering to help people engineer the right processes and the right mindset to take them from point A to point B. He helps people understand the process of creating the right thoughts, and the right action to get the right results."

Seems pretty cut and dry, right? But the capsule of time between chemical engineering and mindset engineering was filled with endless attempts at derailment by the pebble in my shoe.

As an engineer, I was trained to distill crude oil and transform it into gasoline. However, in the early to mid-stages of my

"Inventure" (my inward journey towards fulfilling my life's work), I was the crude, unprocessed, raw, confused, foggy— Ray with ore (pebble) in my shoe.

I answered my call and went from totally left brain (analytical) to totally right brain (creative). And in that transition, all of the linear; logical, scientific principles that I built my life upon were broken down and distilled like that crude oil in a refinery process.

Just as the raw crude is taken through a series of refinery processes (i.e. heat exchangers, fiery furnaces, extractors, distillation, etc.) to produce refined gasoline, my life went through a series of limps, irritants, challenges, failures, and fiery moments, to distill the pride, arrogance, and anger in my shoe.

To this day, my life continues to be refined in my "inventure" towards humility and servant leadership. Observing the moments and purpose of the refiner's fire was key to my transformation.

So, what has your refinery process yielded in your journey?

I remember asking God, "When will these challenges end?"

He responded with the following, "Do you want to be a regular or premium leader?

If you want to be premium grade (as in premium grade gasoline), then you must be willing to go through that fiery furnace several more cycles. If you want to be premium grade, you must discern (observe) and let go and be free of the heavies (the pebble, the oppressive thoughts that are weighing you down, preventing you from showing up in your true light). If you want to be premium grade, you must place yourself under an open heaven and open yourself to new energy that can propel you into a quantum leap and bring you to a state of flow. If you want to be premium grade, ALWAYS, I repeat, ALWAYS remember that I am the Process Design Engineer, and you are the crude."

I mean, what do you say to something like that? It's not like I did not know what was involved in producing premium grade gasoline. I knew exactly the painstaking effort to distill the impurities, the complexities, the obstacles (the pebble, the sludge) and the investment, to be separated in producing premium grade.

I just shook my head, and thought to myself. What a setup! God, you allowed me to observe and experience the natural process of distillation so that I can have grit and resilience as you take me through the transformation process.

So, what have you observed in your natural season that can propel you into your life's calling?

One of the greatest definitions I have ever heard of leadership was from a Harvard professor, which simply said, "Leadership is the distillation of chaos." That's a "drop-the-mic" definition. No wonder I have a passion for leadership.

My life now has been a walking, living parable— a metaphor, if you will— of my professional training as a process design engineer. But I am not unique. You too can live a life as a walking parable as you observe the deeper meaning of each moment along your professional journey.

I have heard it many times before, but I am convinced more than ever now, that life is to be lived twice: first the natural, then the spiritual. I am also convinced that life is not meant to be a discovering, but an unveiling, and the unveiling is through the observance of our own seasons of distillation and refinement.

I observed something in South Africa that was the turning point in my journey from arrogance to humility. I was on a mission trip during the same time of September 11. When the plane crashed into the towers, all international flights ceased and US citizens were warned to stay off the streets.

All plans for ministry and mission were out the window. Instead of giving, I found myself receiving from members of the Indian nation in South Africa. They brought meals to our group three times a day. They knew we were sequestered and were under strict instruction from the US Embassy to stay within the confines of the hotel.

I never experienced this type of love from the Indian race before. As a matter of fact, as a kid growing up in the Caribbean, the racial prejudice was between Blacks and Indians. I didn't have to know anything about an Indian person as a child. Walls would immediately go up whenever I encountered a person of Indian descent.

I never knew I was prejudiced. Until South Africa.

It's been said that "the worst type of arrogance is the arrogance of ignorance." Well there I was, in probably the worst type of prejudice; the prejudice of ignorance. But the more I received love, the deeper the root of prejudice was plucked up. Though I had no idea how, where, or when those seeds of prejudice were sown into me as a child, the Indian tribe in South Africa was the mirror that caused me to see (observe) who I truly was.

It was in my journey from arrogance to humility. There have been people who have caused me to observe the seeds of pride that, more often than not, I was unaware how or when they were sown.

What or who has been your mirror that caused you to distinguish (observe) the false from the true, and pull up those twisted images of yourself?

What's the irritant in your shoe that's yet to be observed and unveiled, and has made you to walk with a limp in your natural life? My friend and mentor, Lisa Nichols has a saying, "All you need is one reason to move forward." Whatever your reason is, rest assured, that reason will cause you to observe the pain and discomfort and move forward in spite of the pebble in your shoe.

Chapter Four:
What's in "Your" S.H.O.E. – Emotional Intelligence (EQ)

IQ is in my head, but EQ is in my feet.

After an 18-hour flight and overcoming jet lag, I was ready to deliver my talk to a group of CEOs in downtown Melbourne, Australia. What I was not ready for was the greeting by a middle-aged lady who stood patiently near the steps that led to the stage. As I was about to make my way onto the first step, she extended her hand and I politely extended mine to shake hers. She then gripped my hands, moved closer towards me and whispered, "We may look like you, we may talk like you, but I want you to know one thing: we are not like you." Then she released her hands, as if to say, "I'm done!"

All I could think of in that moment was, "There's no way I'm going to travel THIS FAR to serve this illustrious group only to be derailed by an obstacle at the point of delivering this baby." The speech went very well. I spoke to the heart of leadership.

At the end of my talk who did I see at the end of the steps? You guessed it, the same middle aged lady. I said to myself, "You've got to be kidding me!" I turned to my right for an alternate exit but quickly decided to face this head on.

As I got midway down the steps I noticed something different. Her countenance had changed. Once again, she extended her hands, and once again, I extended mine. This time she did not draw closer to me, this time she drew closer AND hugged me and whispered, "Please forgive me. I misjudged you (American Businesses). I stereotyped you, but you are different."

This was one of my greatest lessons on the importance of Self Awareness (one of the principles of Emotional Intelligence). I have vowed to develop and keep that trait in my S.H.O.E.

Fast forward, almost a decade later, around 5 PM on a Friday afternoon, after traveling through five cities in five days, I was pretty wiped out and was looking forward to lying in my own bed. Conditions appeared favorable for this to happen. There was, oddly enough, very little traffic on this rush hour Friday. I made it to Milwaukee airport in record time. I even had time to stop at Burger King on my way to the airport for one of their new Chili Dogs. Upon arrival, I realized I could get on an earlier flight if I were to go on standby.

As I approached the ticket counter, I said, "Good evening." No response, no acknowledgement, not even a nod of the head. I kept my composure and waited for the ticket agent to acknowledge me. She finally said, "Can I help you?" in a not so helpful tone.

I responded with sheer joy, "Actually, I'm hoping you can assist me in getting on the standby for the 5:45 PM flight."

Never in a million years could I have anticipated her response. She responded, "Sir, this is Milwaukee, it is what it is!"

With a blank stare on my face I responded, "Thank you so much, since I'm already here, if you could check me in on my originally scheduled 7:30 PM flight I would really appreciate it."

She reluctantly did, and with that I received my boarding pass and walked away.

After three footsteps I turned around and said, "One more thing, you wouldn't happen to have any sanitizer gel, would you? I stopped for a hotdog at Burger King on the way to the airport, and as I was driving I spilled some mustard on my suit."

With lightning speed, she left the ticket counter, went in the back to their storage facility, got me some sanitizer and a face towel. She said, "You don't want to use paper towel because you will mess up your suit."

I stood there in shock, watching this metamorphosis right before my eyes, asking myself, "Is this the same person who spoke rudely to me less than two minutes ago?"

What just happened there? Some would say, "You got her to think on something other than her job. You appealed to her human side. You connected with her. You approached her in a way she never expected. She probably thought you were coming back to light her up."

Dr. Seuss once said:

You have brains in your head. You have feet in your shoes. You can steer yourself any direction you choose. You're on your own. And you know what you know. And YOU are the one who'll decide where to go.

This quote is profound, particularly the part that says, "You can [with head and feet] steer yourself in any direction you choose." Certainly, this scenario at the Milwaukee airport could have steered me in a much different direction, but I am so glad that my feet took me down the path of emotional intelligence, personal character, and integrity, instead of retaliation.

Over the ensuing months, I began to notice similar patterns and results. Allow me to highlight two more scenarios.

February 13, 2017. I was facilitating a leadership workshop in New Orleans. I was fortunate enough to have my wife with me on this trip. Because my workshops are all day, I typically request a late checkout at my hotels so that I can rest my feet during the lunch break. So, I was quite shocked when I got to my room and my wife stated that housekeeping kept knocking at the door, even though there clearly was a do-not-disturb sign on the outside door handle.

It got worse. While I was enjoying my meal, a staff member did not even knock but actually barged into the room. At this point I am saying to myself, "This cannot be happening."

I said to the staff member, "Ma'am, we have a late checkout. How many times do we have to say that? Furthermore, do you really think it is acceptable to barge into a guest room without knocking, especially, with a do-not-disturb sign on the handle?" After that, I gave up all hope of relaxing before heading back to the afternoon session of my workshop. I immediately called the front desk and requested a face-to-face meeting with the hotel manager.

As I got out of the elevator, the manager was waiting for me and his face was red and his hands clenched. I knew he was expecting an explosive outburst. I said to him, "I only have a few minutes before I begin my afternoon session. During my lunch break, I had one goal in mind and that was to relax. It has been far from a relaxing period because of the series of disturbances by your staff. I'm not looking to get anything from you, I am not asking you to comp my room or provide me a discount because of the inconvenience, but what I do ask is that you look into this.

Clearly this is a systemic issue (a communication breakdown) between the front desk and housekeeping. The main reason we are having this conversation is because I do not want the next guest after me to experience what I just went through."

He looked at me as though he had seen a ghost. He was expecting an explosive outburst, but instead, he received assertiveness, tactfulness, and professionalism. I thanked him for listening, then I headed swiftly to my afternoon session.

The following day (Valentine's Day) I received a call from the front desk. To my surprise the front desk stated, "Mr. Charles, our hotel manager, who you spoke to yesterday is not here today, however he left strict instructions to call you first thing in the morning to inform you that you have been upgraded to the presidential suite. Happy Valentine's Day."

Wow.

Emotional intelligence, communicating with tact, professionalism, and assertiveness does have its privileges.

The final scenario I would like to share occurred at 8:55 AM (five minutes before the beginning of another one of my leadership workshops.) As I was approaching the podium, I was intercepted by one of the attendees who was every bit of 6 feet, seven inches, 280 pounds. The first thing he said to me was, "You guys don't serve coffee here?"

"No sir."

That definitely did not go over well with him. He responded, "You guys should make that clearer in your invitations, don't you think?"

"We will take that under advisement," I responded. About a minute after this exchange, I heard my inner voice say, "Just run upstairs to the restaurant and get the man a cup of coffee." I looked around to see who that voice addressed. Clearly, it could not possibly be me; not after that rude display. I heard the voice again, and I knew I was being stretched beyond the point of right vs. wrong.

I made a dash to the restaurant, picked up coffee, an assortment of flavored and unflavored cream and sweeteners and delivered it to the irate attendee with less than a minute to spare to start time.

"All you need is one reason to move forward."

My motive was not to impress him but to simply be obedient to the voice of my conscience (empathy in the midst of insolence). As I delivered the coffee to him he said, "Man, you didn't have to do that."

I responded, "I know I didn't have to. Enjoy!"

What happened next has forever altered my view on hostility.

Just before the afternoon session started, the "irate customer" came up to me, and I thought, "Oh no, here we go again."

This time it was different. This time he said, "Ray where were you, I looked everywhere for you at our lunch break. I wanted to treat you to lunch."

This time we switched roles. This time I said, "Oh man, you didn't have to do that."

He responded, "I know I didn't have to, but I wanted to." This guy turned out to be one of my most engaged students all day.

As in the previous three scenarios, my feet took me down the path of pure motives versus the path of entitlement and rights. The results each and every time was enchantment from a place of hostility.

I had no idea that my feet were walking out the various components of Emotional Intelligence:

Social Skills

Personal Character

Integrity

Motivation

Good Communication

Relational Skills

Personal Management

So, as we bring this chapter to a close, I ask the same question as I have done previously, "What's in YOUR shoe?" Is it skill, experience and general intelligence, or is it skill, experience and a combination of general experience and emotional intelligence?

Chapter Five:
Next Steps

If you really want to know what's in your S.H.O.E.:

- Spirit

- Habits

- Observant

- Emotional Intelligence (EQ)

I encourage you to listen to what people are saying, feeling, and hearing when you appear in person, on the phone or in writing. If someone says to you, for example, "When you come into my presence, I see light, I feel a sense of peace in your presence," that's a good indication that life (and everything that life represents) is in your shoe.

Here is a four simple exercises you can practice to sharpen your sensory acuity of what's in your shoe.

Exercise #1

Ask five to ten of your friends, "What's the first thing you think of when you hear my name?" Listen for the patterns.

Exercise #2

Have an "if you really knew me session" with five to ten of your colleagues. In other words, share with your friends 5-10 different variations of the following statement:

"If you really knew me, you would know that _____" Document your statements and, again, watch for the patterns and their reaction.

Exercise #3

Answer this very simple question, "What's important to you?" (at least 25 times). After you have written down your final answer truncate your list to your top three. Chances are they are the governing forces that are shaping the context of what's in your shoe.

Exercise #4

My friend Lisa Nichols created a powerful mirroring exercise that is a perfect tool to uncover what's in your shoe. For a minimum of 21 days, position yourself each day in the mirror and go seven layers deep by completing the following:

- I am proud that you ......
- I forgive you for ....
- I commit to you that ......

This is certainly not an all-inclusive list, but what you will discover as you complete these self-work tasks is that you will be more conscious of your unique story that you are writing each and every day with YOUR feet in your shoe. Moreover, you will become more acutely aware of the overcoming forces of the pebble that's in your shoe.

Next Steps with Dr. Ray

What's the value you received from reading through this book? Go ahead and write it down. Name three things you can see yourself implementing in the next 24 - 48 hours. If the value you've already gained is reason enough to gain deeper insight and breakthrough to the four elements of what's in your S.H.O.E., then I encourage you if you haven't already done so, to join our mailing list by visiting DrRayCharles.com and become a member of our Facebook group, "Enough IS Enough: What's In "Your" S.H.O.E." This group will always have the first right of refusal to any e-Courses, Webinars, Live workshops, etc.

I am humbled to serve you through the many characters in this book.

Each time you put on your shoe, I trust that a thought, a story, a character, from this book will cause you to move forward. Your Spirit, Habits, Observations, and Emotional Intelligence, via your inner voice and Distinct Natural Ability, are what propels you from one place to the next, from here, to there. Identify the pebbles that are in YOUR S.H.O.E., and move forward in victory.

Yes, this is more than a Long Walk to Freedom. Rather, this is your Faith Walk of Victory. Let's go!

Remember: "It only takes one reason to move forward." -Lisa Nichols

Made in the USA
Lexington, KY
02 July 2018